WHAT PEOPLE ARE SAYING ABOUT

Being Enough

"Seldom have I had the pleasure of reading passages written with such grace, precision and power. Leigh Sanders is a new voice that helps us see beyond our self-imposed limitations of fear and anxiety to a new realm of wholeness and love."

—H. Jackson Brown, Jr.
author of *Life's Little Instruction Book* and *Live and Learn and Pass It On*

"Leigh Sanders captures the yearning we feel to believe that life has purpose and that we measure up even when circumstances would have us believe otherwise. I found myself feeling his healing words reach deep into my very soul and heal the unspoken loneliness and lack of self-belief that seems inexorably tied to our human condition.

"Leigh's words and moving photographs bring hope and sustenance to our busy lives. His words encourage us to look at our efforts with renewed wonder and self-belief, realizing again that indeed we are enough."

—Meredith Young-Sowers
author of *Agartha: A Journey to the Stars* and *Angelic Messenger Cards*

"Turning the pages of Leigh Sanders' exquisitely beautiful book is wonderful experience to really knowing what being natural is. It is th wonderful unification of thought and feelings, words and pictures. An to know that to be natural is to become more and more what 'natur intends us humans to BE."

—Tom Malone, Ph.D., M.
coauthor of *The Art of Intimacy* and *Windows of Experie*

"A wise and lovely book."

—Carol Orsbc
author of *The Art of Resili*

"The author speaks of the inevitability of change, of the distress plans interrupted, ambitions obstructed, failures suffered. He confror reality, and deals with it by producing a volume of inspiratior thoughts. His words, though weighty, are few; images of nature cor plete his meditations. . . . Drawing lessons from the turning of t seasons, he invites the reader to consider the value of a fallow time, wh all is subdued, sounds muffled, colors muted—the time of great inwa work. . . . He comes to believe, and is here to persuade the contempl tive reader, that there is order in the world, that life is the journey mc than the destination, but that the right path leads us home."

—Margie Weath
columnist, *Smoky Mountain Sentinel & Business R*

Being Enough

The Answers We Seek Are All Around Us

LEIGH SANDERS

Health Communications, Inc.
Deerfield Beach, Florida

www.bci-online.com

Library of Congress Cataloging-in-Publication Data

Sanders, Leigh, date.
   Being enough : the answers we seek are all around us / Leigh Sanders.
     p.   cm.
   ISBN 1-55874-909-8 (pbk.)
     1. Meditations.   2. Nature—Religious aspects—Meditations.   I. Title.

BL624.2 .S26 2001
158.1'28—dc21   00-050597

©2001 Leigh Sanders
ISBN 1-55874-909-8

HCI, its Logos and Marks are trademarks of Health Communications, Inc.

Publisher: Health Communications, Inc.
           3201 S.W. 15th Street
           Deerfield Beach, FL 33442-8190

Photography by Leigh Sanders
Cover and inside book design by Lawna Patterson Oldfield

Contents

Acknowledgments...vii

Introduction ix

PART I

The River Waits..3

In the Quiet—An Assurance...19

Times of Gray 35

Being Enough 49

The Greenness 69

PART II

I Am 83

Just to Be a Part of It...............................97

The Leaves in Our Lives............................111

But Have You Asked for Help? 131

How Wonderful! 151

PART III

Neptune...167

The Magic of the Mountain..........................181

Thanksgiving 189

Your Harvest 199

At Christmas Time 217

Acknowledgments

When we live life in good faith, aware of our limitations and lack of control, the universe sends angels and sages to us in response to our pleas for help. Over the years I was writing *Being Enough,* my life became blessed with these people, and I wish to publicly thank them.

Dr. Tom Malone: I always see the word *master* when I think of Tom Malone. Master of words, master of human nature, master of being. He has been a teacher and guide to me for years and years. Now that he has retired, I miss him so. There are beacons in the night, guiding us to safe harbor, to moorings in our consciousness that are everlasting points of reference and strength. Tom Malone, for myself and hundreds of others, has been such a beacon. Since the 1950s, Tom has been plowing new ground in psychiatry and planting it with new information, new approaches to health, and the world is a better place for it. And so, thank God, am I.

Karen Branch: First my counselor, then my friend, and now my companion. Karen is that person whose presence in my life elevates all my perceptions, whose energy inspires my confidence and my growth. And whose love sustains me. No trail is ever more exhilarating, no vista more captivating, than when Karen is there. No picture or writing is ever more satisfying, more meaningful to me, than when I first share it with Karen. She is the pool in my life's river. And she carefully led me to the realization that we are all "enough."

Introduction

Change comes to all of us. Interruptions in our worldly plans, obstacles to our ambitions. And failures come. Failures in our relationships and in our expectations of outer-world success. All of these are the phenomena of change, self-conflict and self-doubt.

Six or seven years ago, I encountered all of these challenges. These difficult conditions quickly tested my notion of who I really was.

This time required, no, demanded that I examine how I defined myself, what I believed about God, about me, and about life and death. And this time required that I decide how I would choose to live and die.

I looked for help in all the places our culture expects to find it in times like this—psychiatry, astrology, meditation, religious teachings, yoga and books, lots of books. Books of all the current thinking on holistic self-concepts, self-analysis and awareness.

For years I dutifully explored the dark side of my person, which was that part of me most often present. Gratefully, I found no analytical contradictions, regardless the approach to self. It increasingly seemed to me that truth rested at the center of all life, and all paths to enlightenment led, like spokes in a cosmic wheel, to that truth.

Then, on a trip to see yet another of God's way-showers, I revisited the mountains of western North Carolina, the towns of Murphy, Hayesville, Franklin, Bryson City, Fontana, Robbinsville and Andrews. And I visited the wonderful reaches of the Nantahala National

Forest with its hundreds of miles of gravel roads that wind deep into the heart of that mountain range.

As I rode for days on end in my truck, I began to feel in the natural surroundings a sense of assurance, a oneness with the natural world that became to me an affirmation of the worthiness of life, all life, my life. It was then, in 1994, that I began to write down for the very first time what I was hearing and feeling and to take pictures of the scenes that inspired these thoughts. I hiked, I camped, sat on remote mountain tops, explored whole mountain ranges off any beaten trail. I couldn't get close enough to all this natural abundance. The result was a continuous confirmation of the simple beauty of life without everyday struggle and without annual agendas.

I have written down these thoughts for me. As soon as I would decide that my reflections pertained to a past difficulty, I would encounter a life passage to which the piece was even more appropriate. A lifetime friend observed that I was getting the answers before God gave me the test. And I am so grateful for that.

I share this book with you in the faith that these reflections will connect you with that part of you that holds your strength and unconditional compassion for yourself, the seat of your self-love and irrevocable self-approval. And I know that person you so want to be will surely meet you somewhere along this wonderful path.

PART 1

The River Waits

Effortlessly the stream
cascades down the face of
the mountain.

Willingly moving aside as it
passes the giant boulders that sit
obstinately in its path.

Patiently it waits in pools
as the terrain levels in the stream's path,
not wishing to move any more
quickly than is natural.

Content just to be in this
one place, grateful for the experience.
Trusting, as it waits, that the next
passage will unfold
as it should.

Knowing only that the river
waits below, that the destination
is assured. And no moment is scarred
with the fear that the stream's path
is somehow unsafe ahead.

Because the spirit that is
the stream is constant, continuous and
worthy of the trust it enjoys.

Would that we could live like this!

Effortlessly meeting the new day,
as our life sometimes cascades ahead
of us in bursts of changing
circumstance.

Willingly confronting the obstacles
in our lives and avoiding the temptation
to paint them as problems.
Choosing rather to savor the rush
of spontaneity they can introduce in our
experience of this particular time.

Patiently abiding the periods in
our life passage during which activity
wanes, visible progress ceases and we
have only to wait for our good to
appear without struggle.

Content to be in this moment,
blessing the process and accepting
the past with quiet gratitude.

Always trusting that
the unknown, the unseen territory
in our lives ahead will manifest in a manner
that will support us, nurture us, expand
our spirit and allow us the room to grow.
Knowing only that, in the current
of universal energy in which we bathe
and flow, the destination is assured.
The peace we deserve and the love we
seek will come to us, when it will,
as it will, as abundantly
as we dreamed.

For we are safe within the spirit
of this life stream.

It is continuous, constant
and worthy of our faith. Too often
forgetting this, we try too hard to control
the flow and change the course.
And we trust too little that life will unfold
for us in a way that will reward
our faith with wholeness
and completion.

But in the silence and serenity
of the pools in our lives, we can know
that always, always the
river waits below.

And then we can feel from
the depths of our being that our
destination in peace
is assured.

In the Quiet—
An Assurance

Be still now and
listen to the silence.

Winter comes and with it
the day's light isn't
with us for long.

The trees,
barren against the brown
of the mountain's cover,
don't speak now.

The streams even seem muffled,
less exuberant in their trek
down the mountain.

Dry leaves rustling with
the sound of deer foraging,
but very quietly.

This is a time of
nature's introspection,
of going within and
conserving strength.

The universe knows how
to use this time and
so should we.

We must trust that in
these times when our brilliance fades
and our colors dim, that internally,
great work is taking place, beyond
our perception, out beyond
our consciousness.

These are the moments on
which our future growth depends.

The strength we will express,
the personal power in our future life,
will begin here in the quiet.

So be still now.
Trust.
Feel the grace of this time
and know
that you are growing
—even now.

Times of Gray

Gray clouds promising snow.
Gray winds that drive the winter's cold
swiftly down the valley.
Brown grass lying close to the ground
in the long pasture, as ice begins
to cover the stream along
the mountain road.

Gray days happen in winter,
shutting out the sun.
Closing us off from the warmth and
the light, driving us to shelter.

Yet occasionally, even during
times like this, the clouds break.
Then the sun's brilliance explodes into
our view, creating a wondrous bouquet of
every tree in the great hardwoods on
the mountain. Painting a shimmering
silver image that captures every
limb for just a moment.

Where seconds before
everything was dull and gray,
now there is brilliant definition in
wonderful, sparkling detail.

And we are amazed as we realize
it was there all the time.

Spiritual enlightenment
happens much the same
way in our lives.

It comes to us only after
long periods of difficulty that seem to
chill our sensitivity to everything.
Times that drive us away from our
concept of who we are and
deny us our being.

Yet when truth does come to us,
it suddenly paints our life
with meaning.

Illuminating the complexity in
our experience, bringing understanding
where before there was only
gray confusion.

And we endure the harshness
of our emotional winters by holding
to the images uncovered by those divine
bursts of awareness. We survive with
the warmth of that meaning captured in
our soul space, sheltering us from
the cold confusion blowing down
the valleys of our lives.

And, sitting with our
backs to the cold, harsh wind of
our experience, we hold to that memory,
knowing the meaning, the purpose
in our life, is there all the time.
Just waiting for us to awaken to our
own capacity to comprehend and
to find enduring peace in that
sacred understanding.

Being Enough

In its normal, undisturbed state,
nature is always enough.

There is always enough sunlight.
There are always enough trees in the
forest. There are always enough
mountains to shelter the valleys.
There is always enough natural food
for the animals and enough water
in the streams. And the eagle always
flies high enough on wings that
are always strong enough.

And in all this glorious,
natural world, nothing more is required
for the mountains, forest, and
all that abide there, to be
all God intended.

They are enough.

But as we, in the hurry and
struggle of our lives, put ever greater
distances between ourselves and our
true nature, we tend to forget
that we too are enough.

In our striving to prove
ourselves, to compete, to please,
to succeed, we lose touch with
our own adequacy and our
natural wholeness.
And why?

Most often because we are
attempting to live a truth that is not ours,
to follow a path that is not natural for us.
We bend, stretch and reach beyond
our grasp to achieve, to perform.
But for whom?

And then, there are those
among us, men and women we encounter,
who are being enough. The writer who
finds the words without struggle.
The composer-musician for whom the
melody is everlasting. The teacher who
conveys the message with such
ease and thoroughness.

And we say of them,
"They were meant to do that;
it comes to them so naturally."

Yes. Because they are
living in the center of their truth.
And so can each of us live at
the epicenter of our truth.

But how?

First, by accepting what we are not.

We are not defined by the
measure of our material, professional
success and achievement; we
are bigger than that.

We are not forever obligated to
careers outside our truth; we are broader
than that. We are not required to wager
our personhood in an attempt to
please anyone; we are more
precious than that.

So listen in faith within to hear the
song that is uniquely you.

And remember as you do there are
enough trees, not one too many.

Whatever your gift, your task, it is
precisely what is needed.

Here? Yes, here. Now? Right now.

Listen to your song and move your life to its tempo. That is the melody that only you can sing and that all the world wants to hear.

Because you too are enough. Enough to fill the universal space reserved especially for your spirit. Accept it, own it and leave the other tunes to someone else.

For like all the rest of nature,
as you are about being, being enough—
you will discover that nothing more
is required of you to be just as
perfect as God intended.

There is great freedom in that.

For you were born to that energy.

Your life, from the very first moment,
was tuned to that melody.
Your intuition knows every note.
Your spirit feels its compelling tempo.

Flow with it like the rushing stream.
Soar with it on eagle's wings.

Listen to your song and join the dance.
Live in the center of your truth
and find the bliss of always
being enough.

The Greenness

Lush, moist, fresh.
The greenness of spring arrives
on the mountain in urgent waves of
foliage, expanding daily to cover more
of the bare structure that was there
before, completing the mountain's
profile in rushes of green,
every imaginable shade
of green.

This is the green of
new growth. The tenderness,
the subtlety of spring, silently arriving
in fresh, crisp, sunlit mornings,
anointed with the soft scent of all
the wild flowering, adorned with
blossoms drenched
in dew.

Look carefully in the
early light.

This is your awakening.

This is your spring.

This is the unfolding of your growth
after a season of quiet
spent patiently.

Here is the expression
of your new strength, your power
to manifest the wonder of
your unique spirit.

You have stored your energy
for a time. Now you find the expression
of your person in fresh, new activity.
And every morning now, your
new announcement of life fills you,
asserting your wholeness, the
essence of your being.

This is the beginning.
A season to enjoy the natural
abundance of all that you
are becoming,
all that you deserve.

And these are the
first signs of the wonderful
promise that your future holds, as
you complete the spiritual structure
your struggle has carved
for your life.

And God smiles as
you experience the grand rebirth
of your spirit, the greenness
of your personal
spring.

PART II .

I Am

I am always safe
—safe in the knowledge of
my connection to the God
within and His wisdom,
His plan for me.

I am never alone—
never out of reach of the divine
energy in which my soul immerses
itself, renewing its
strength.

I am always in the present—
the location of my power to cocreate
with the universe—to lock arms
with God and maximize my
life experience.

I am out of fear and doubt—
knowing the impact those feelings
have on my creative self, knowing they
are not part of who I am, only
where I have been.

I am thoroughly in love with me—
honoring who I am today, blessing my
progress and supporting my quest
to serve and my deservedness
to receive.

I am free—free because
I have awakened to my lack of control.
Letting go of my attachment to the
outcomes—holding only to the quality of
the spiritual growth and the richness
of the life experience.

I am in good faith.
Faith that holds firmly to the
abundance that is ours,
to the joy that we allow in our now,
to the love that we must only
give in order to receive.

I am worthy—
worthy of the completion of
good in my life.
Letting that happen to me in the way
God intends, when He intends,
and knowing with clarity
that He does.

I am aware—aware of how
important it is every day to be all that
I am, filling myself with that day's
experience and knowing that even the
struggle carries with it an
expression of God's perfect
plan for me.

I am growing—
growing in my spiritual
comprehension of the wonder
of it all, and the grace that awaits the
letting go. It waits only on my
affirmation of me to
nurture me.

And that affirmation
is simply,
I am.

Just to Be a
Part of It

The robin sings
as it wings into the sunrise.
The oak stretches as the dawn's
rays fall on its long branches.
The brook dances
in the delicate morning light.
And all are satisfied to share this
experience of life.
Just to be a robin, an oak, a brook.
Just to be a part of it.

And yet, we spend
our lives attempting to be different.
Trying to set ourselves above the rest,
as ambition, pride and ego hold
us in their steel-like grip.
We have come to believe that
our definition lies in excelling. And so,
we are caught in the continuous
comparison of our accomplishments.
Desperately trying to separate
ourselves, lest we be somehow lost
in some faceless crowd.

And then we sit with
a friend in that distress that
erases all pretension. We listen to
their deepest feelings as they
express the life that's touching them.
And, as we hear the strong, deep
lyrics of their being, we hear
in the background the harmony
of our own experience.
Then we come closer.
For we realize the melody we
follow is the same.

While we are striving
to be so different, we miss the
chance to share the wonder of this life.
Our real challenge lies in finding the
capacity to understand, touching
that natural freedom in us that permits
our total honesty with others.
Then our pride falls away
of its own weight.

Only then do we find
the completion that comes with
sharing unashamed the life
that we all are living.
And over and over again
we discover that the really important
pieces of our lives are not the
things we thought.
The golden moments that set us
free are found when
we are just being
a part of it.

The robin,
the oak, the brook,
you and me.

The Leaves in Our Lives

There are great messages
in nature in each fall of our years,
displayed first to our eyes and
spoken to our souls as well
if we are listening.

The months pass
and our expectations are
aroused as the leaves on the
mountains begin to
change.

Green merging to
gold and crimson, first slowly—
then suddenly with great
momentum in a crescendo of
glorious color.

And the hills are alive
with their fleeting brilliance.
It is all at once wonderful,
exhilarating and always
new to us.

And yet what is the meaning,
the significance in those brief weeks
of nature's autumn
excitement?

Growth!
Growth in our lives brings change.
Slowly at first,
but during some seasons of our time,
rapid, frightening, glorious,
painful change.

Then our brilliance appears,
brand-new again, erupting into color
in our experience, celebrating our growth.
And each year of our progress is
uniquely new and surprisingly
beautiful.

For it is not the
singular intention of the tree
to be arrayed in a cascade of color.
That splendid display is
incidental, a punctuation of the more
lasting experience of growth,
the expression of
nature's universal truth.

In our own lives,
when we allow our egos to judge
for us what is truly important,
too often we assign more meaning to
the fleeting brilliance in our existence.
Holding to it, fearing it will not last.
Striving to reproduce it even when
our inner spirit's growth is unattended,
the victim of our tedium
and struggle.

And then, we let our egos chase
the color in life while we ignore
our only real task.

We simply must grow
and change, moving through our
seasons, to have a complete experience
of life in all its dimensions.
For the real glory of our landscape
is found in our gradual and continuous
effort to find the path
to growth.

We know that the
moments of brilliance will come
if we live life every day for its own sake,
simply asserting our truth.
Then effortlessly like the leaves,
life will announce another
autumn's foliage.

And just as the changing leaf
is the tree's unique choice of adornment
in its celebration of growth,
so it is for us.
As we replace the ego's enthusiasm
for appearances with the soul's passion
for the expansion of our spirit,
again and again, our true
colors arrive.

Then with rhythmic regularity,
the seasons of our lives share
with us their rewards.
Wholeness, completion and rebirth
come as freely as the gold and
crimson that joyously appear
in the grand celebration
on the mountain.

But Have You Asked for Help?

Only in the sun's light
does growth come to the wilderness.
Only then do leaves grow, bees
roam, flowers bloom.
And only in the darkness do
the creatures rest, does the forest cool
and energy regenerates in all
that flourishes there.
And in every moment, light or dark,
they are each assisted by that energy
that brought life to them, designed
their existence, filled them
with purpose.

In your life,
there is a natural plan.
A plan for your growth, your
nourishment, your silence,
your rest and restoration.
And the cycles that bring the
darkness and the light revolve
through your life without
your conscious effort.

Moving you,
inspiring you,
shaping you.

And yet,
how troubled you become
when your plans seem to fail,
when your ambitions meet obstruction.
For somewhere, sometime along
this path, you have come to believe
that the plan depends entirely on you;
that control is the sign of your
mastery of this life;
that your management of
your experience signals some
maturity in your journey.
But have you asked for help?

Where is the natural harmony
you seek with that energy
that created you?
Where is there room in this plan
of yours for the assistance you need,
the nourishment that life can bring
to you so effortlessly?
Are you open to that help?

For in the plan of the all that is,
there is provision for your safety,
your growth and your natural abundance.
The light that fills the wilderness with
spring fills you with energy and insight.
The darkness plans your rest.

But there must be
a time for allowing, times of
accepting the natural cycles in
your experience.
And times when you
trust enough to release your
insistence on control of
all of this.

For when you do
consciously acknowledge your
need, help will come to you as
naturally as it is available
to all other living things,
in the time and way
intended.

For you too were
meant to be safe; you too
were intended to grow
and flourish.
And, at times,
you were meant to rest
from all of this.

Have you asked
for help?

How Wonderful!

How wonderful
these pinnacles of green
rising around me now!
They send my spirit soaring, bursting
through the mist of my memories,
losing my fears effortlessly like
kite tails drifting away.

I breathe in life as freely
as the wind that clears
the rain from the
valley below.

I am the calm
that holds the cloud
against the mountainside,
hiding its peak.

I feel the strength of these
great hills; their power quietly shelters
me against that part of life
that overwhelms.
They accept my weakness,
forgiving my doubt that the
storm would pass.

My fate twists like the road ahead,
and yet tomorrow. . . .

Tomorrow breaks into a promise
as brilliant as the rainbow that
appears in the wake
of the thunder.

God's abundance showers
from the greenness,
the wholeness of this natural
spectacle and gives my soul the
space it needs to take
the mountains in.

Then my release comes
and I surrender to it.
The tears flow, healing my
wounds as the hills hold
my silence.

Yes . . . yes.

God's truth flows through me
here in this place.
I feel him come to me as surely
and quietly as the streams
seek the bed of the
river in the valley.

And nothing is required
of me here, only that I continue
to be silent and listen and
watch the fullness of the
August moon.

How wonderful!

PART III

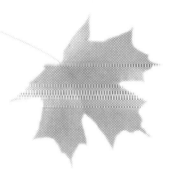

Neptune

Beneath the surface of
my conscious mind
lie all the treasures
of the universe.

The truths,
the inspirations, the revelations.
All available if I will only be quiet
and ask that they
speak to me.

But I must first
abandon my knowing,
my judgment,
my attachment to
particular outcomes and
conclusions.

My ego must stand aside
as well, and give up its assertion
of my personality,
allowing my higher self to emerge
as the active participant
in the exchange.

Then freedom occurs.
The freedom to hear,
the freedom from fear of
what I will hear,
the freedom to surrender to
my truth and my good
in whatever form it
may manifest.

Living the questions,
but also allowing the answers
to live themselves out
in my life.

The Magic of the Mountain

As God's creations,
when we are immersed in the
heart of a primal forest,
we know instinctively that
the outer world
doesn't require anything
of us here.

It is here also that
our inner truth speaks to us,
telling us that nothing further
is required of us
to be worthy
of a full life experience.
We must only be open
to receive it.

And looking at
the glory of it all, water, air,
earth, trees, rivers and landscape,
we know that absolutely nothing
more is required of all of this
for it to be as perfect as
God intended—
absolutely nothing.

Thanksgiving

The morning breaks
clear and bright on the pines,
more erect in the crisp air
than usual, it seems.

The cedars are also
paying attention, not quite as
stoic as is their custom.

The fire pops in the
kitchen fireplace as huge biscuits
cook in the old oven again and
yes, this is a different
sort of day.

Regardless of the weight
of yesterday, in spite of the stressful
pressure of current circumstance,
we somehow give ourselves
the permission to just be in this
one morning moment.

And we see with great clarity
what a gift life really is—
just as it is, being only what it is—
right here and now.

Looking only as far ahead as
the abundance of the Thanksgiving meal,
and all the warmth and security that
observing that tradition showers
on our senses; the taste,
the smells, the feelings.

And we bow our hearts
and heads to once again give thanks
for another year of life,
of growth, of experience, and
to bless all that is basic,
modest and sincere about
our lives.

Blessing the things that
are sustainable no matter what.

And in the presence of
this moment we know what is real
and how few things in our lives
are truly important.

And how grand an experience
those few things bring to us every day
as we once again give thanks.

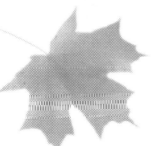

Your Harvest

It is autumn.
The harvest moon breaks into view,
burnt-orange light bathing the bold
Blue Ridge from the east.

And the valley below
is washed clean in its magical glow.

The acres of round bales
stand their watch across newly mowed
fields, casting oblong shadows
toward the farmhouse
to the west.

Rows of corn stand
conspicuously in the silence
beside the stubble of that already
cut and taken.

The last of the crop from
the generous garden by the house
is prepared for the long winter ahead.

And the foliage on the
surrounding mountains begins to
change imperceptibly, giving
just a glimpse of the cascade
of color soon to come.

There are deep feelings
uncovered by the moon's glow.

The strong sense of purpose
in the harvest, the safety we feel
in honest preparation for
more severe times.

The predictability of
another season brings affirmation
of the worthiness of our lives
passing in full color.

The harvests in our lives
are rarely so well-defined in the
rush of the days flying by.

But if we are to lay
by for ourselves in anticipation
of whatever the years will bring,
we must come to that quietness
that is our spiritual and
emotional reserve.

And yet,
where are the silos in our lives?

Where do we find to store
our strength against life's elements?

Look closely and you'll see
where your silo stands.

It stands in the moment
you share honestly that experience
with your child, your friend
or one you love.

Watch as you store that love against
the day that they are away.

It stands in the time you find
to touch the deepest part of you in
quiet meditation, finding that reservoir of
peace that builds in you as you finally
let go and trust in all that's good.

And the silo appears as you
accept in yourself the imperfections
that once frightened and discouraged
you so, and that now the wholeness
of your spirit forgives.

It stands highest in the
humility of your affirmation of
self-love, your tensile strength against
all hardship, the basis of your
personhood, your place
at life's table.

Yes, your harvest is
just as real as that washed in
the glow of the moon and
just as worthy.

It comes from the
same beginnings, preparation,
awareness, honest effort,
perseverance, prayer.

And if you will only be
silent now and then, you'll see
your silo tall, strong, and full of
all you need for any winter
your life encounters.

As your true colors emerge,
like those on the
mountain.

At Christmas Time

Christmas, what is
our experience of Christmas?
As children—surprises, gifts,
an array of things we had wished for
and some we had not.

As parents, a time of
providing, of conforming to role
expectations so thoroughly described
for us over seventy-five years
of commercial attention
to this season.

Another bigger, better Christmas.
More of everything.

More expensive gifts,
more beautiful boxes under
a bigger tree with more lights and
decorations than
last year.

And only then will we
have met our expectations
of Christmas.

Why?

Because we measure our
success as parents by others'
definition of a significant Christmas.
We have thoroughly accepted
the idea that we are deficient,
inadequate and uncaring,
if we haven't supplied
another bigger, better
Christmas.

A certified, quantified, improved
Christmas.

Yet what is the spirit of this time?

The historical event of
Christ's birth is a universal symbol
of God's presence in the midst of men.
Simply, Christ-consciousness
hand-delivered to us with a plain
and powerful message.

The satisfaction
and peace you seek, the
love you need, is in the heart and
soul of each of you waiting
for you to awaken.

Awaken though to what?
To your own complete worthiness
of all the happiness you deserve,
of all the gifts God's spiritual
abundance supplies
without restriction or
discrimination.

There if you will only touch
that place in you and, like a child,
begin again to love the we that
is just God and you.

The real spirit of Christmas
then is compassion.
First for ourselves, displacing
our doubt and despair,
our ego and inadequacy.

And secondly,
our compassion for each other,
accepting the wonderful differences
in our expressions of our lives,
releasing the judgments of
right and wrong,
better or worse . . .

And coming to know
the presence of the Christ spirit in
each of us, emerging, developing,
struggling but ultimately completing us
and fulfilling our uniqueness,
our spirit, our life force and purpose.

So how to accept Christmas then
in all its glitter and pressure for
happiness on demand?

Know that the gifts, large or small,
modest or otherwise, are not incompatible
with the spirit of Christmas.

But they are only the more superficial
expressions of our compassion
for each other.

And they rarely provide
any lasting experience of having
truly shared ourselves, of
having connected in the way we
so hoped we could.
But often, in those moments
during the exchange of material gifts,
words and feelings are exchanged
that carry spiritual,
heartfelt gifts.

Somehow, those are what
we remember.

I thank you
I love you
I respect you
You've helped me so

And then the
compassion in us awakens, for
ourselves and each other, regardless
the content of the packages that
lie unwrapped on the floor
as we speak.

And Christmas arrives again,
soft and strong, quiet and affirming,
reminding us again that we have merged
with our God within and, in the
wonderful truth of that experience,
we have suddenly been completely
available to all of those we
wanted so to love—
at Christmas time.

About the Author

Leigh Sanders is a business consultant who has concentrated his professional activity, for the past 28 years, on managing financially troubled firms back to health.

Leigh is a business graduate of Vanderbilt University. He served as Chairman of the Board of The Heritage School in Newnan, Georgia from 1988-1998, a K-12 college preparatory school on whose Board he has served since 1978.

He lives on a farm in Coweta County about an hour from Atlanta. His family has lived on this farm since the 1860s.

Quiet Your Mind

Eternal Blessings

Blessings are simple yet heartfelt messages that you can bestow on the people you care about, whether you want to remind your spouse of your love, cheer up a coworker who's having a bad day, or comfort a friend facing a trying time you'll find the perfect words in this little gem.

Code #8385 • Quality Paperback • $8.95

Practical Meditation

A peaceful volume that provides a compilation of inspirational passages, exercises and mantras that, when practiced over time, will bring you a sense of clarity, self-awareness and peace of mind.

Code #827X • Quality Paperback • $10.95

... Miracles and Beyond ...

Angel Watch

Bestselling author Catherine Lanigan brings you this provoking and uplifting collection of real-life miracles and reveals how unexplained synchronicity brings positive changes into our lives.

Code #8199 • Quality Paperback • $12.95

One Last Hug Before I Go

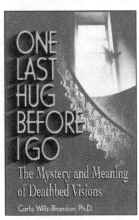

"[This book] widens the door of possibility and offers a new way for Westerners to approach death."
—Publishers Weekly

A groundbreaking book that investigates the phenomenon of the deathbed vision while exploring the eternal question: What happens when we die?

Code #7796 • Quality Paperback • $12.95

True Tales of Strength and Justice

Ultimate Judgment

"A disturbing and compelling story"
—Publishers Weekly

A riveting story of emotional corruption, obsession and betrayal at their darkest levels, but more importantly, a story of human courage, resilience and ultimate triumph.

Code #8318 • Quality Paperback • $12.95

Defending Andy

A powerful memoir of one mother's painful journey to fight against the health care system and try to save her son from cancer.

Code #9063 • Quality Paperback • $12.95

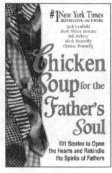